First World War
and Army of Occupation
War Diary
France, Belgium and Germany

3 CAVALRY DIVISION
6 Cavalry Brigade
6 Machine Gun Squadron
29 February 1916 - 31 May 1918

WO95/1152/3

The Naval & Military Press Ltd
www.nmarchive.com
Published in association with The National Archives

Published by

The Naval & Military Press Ltd

Unit 10 Ridgewood Industrial Park,
Uckfield, East Sussex,
TN22 5QE England
Tel: +44 (0) 1825 749494

www.naval-military-press.com

www.nmarchive.com

This diary has been reprinted in facsimile from the original. Any imperfections are inevitably reproduced and the quality may fall short of modern type and cartographic standards.

© **Crown Copyright**
Images reproduced by permission of The National Archives, London, England, 2015.

Contents

Document type	Place/Title	Date From	Date To
Heading	WO95/1152/3 3 Cavalry Division 6 Cavalry Brigade 6 Machine Gun Squadron Feb. 1916-May 1919.		
Heading	3rd Cavalry Division 1916-1919 3rd Cavalry Division 6th Cavalry Brigade 6th Machine Gun Squadron Feb 1916-May 1919		
War Diary	Offin (Pdic)	29/02/1916	29/02/1916
War Diary	Offin	21/03/1916	21/03/1916
War Diary	Letouquet	01/05/1916	26/06/1916
War Diary	Bonnay	27/06/1916	30/06/1916
War Diary	Le Touquet	11/06/1916	30/06/1916
War Diary	Bonnay	01/07/1916	31/07/1916
War Diary	La Neuville	01/08/1916	01/08/1916
War Diary	Cavron St Martin	05/08/1916	26/08/1916
War Diary	Cavron	25/08/1916	30/08/1916
War Diary	Beaumon Hamel Thiepval area in part line in Support	03/09/1916	10/09/1916
War Diary	N B.	05/09/1916	21/10/1916
War Diary	Verton	01/11/1916	22/12/1916
War Diary	Maresquel	22/12/1916	22/12/1916
War Diary	Verton	11/12/1916	14/12/1916
War Diary	Maresquel	14/12/1916	14/12/1916
War Diary	Maresquel Ecquemicourt	01/01/1917	30/01/1917
War Diary	Souchez	01/02/1917	28/02/1917
War Diary	Villers-au-Bois	01/03/1917	01/03/1917
War Diary	Maresquel	02/03/1917	02/03/1917
War Diary	Cabaret Rouge	01/03/1917	01/03/1917
War Diary	Maresquel	02/03/1917	05/04/1917
War Diary	Vacquerie	07/04/1917	07/04/1917
War Diary	Fosseux	08/04/1917	08/04/1917
War Diary	Arras	09/04/1917	09/04/1917
War Diary	Duisans and Arras	10/04/1917	10/04/1917
War Diary	Arras	11/04/1917	12/04/1917
War Diary	Fosseux	12/04/1917	12/04/1917
War Diary	Vaulx	16/04/1917	20/04/1917
War Diary	Buire-Le-Sec	20/04/1917	19/05/1917
War Diary	Buire	22/05/1917	23/05/1917
War Diary	Epehy	01/05/1917	22/05/1917
War Diary	Buire	02/06/1917	10/06/1917
War Diary	Epehy	10/06/1917	28/06/1917
War Diary	Buire	01/07/1917	03/07/1917
War Diary	Auchel	04/07/1917	17/07/1917
War Diary	Le Touquet	18/07/1917	30/09/1917
War Diary	Haverskerque (Le Touquet)	01/10/1917	27/10/1917
War Diary	Epaene	01/11/1917	30/11/1917
War Diary	Rubempre	01/12/1917	31/12/1917
War Diary	Epagne	02/01/1918	27/01/1918
War Diary	Argoeuves	28/01/1918	28/01/1918
War Diary	Harbonniers	29/01/1918	29/01/1918
War Diary	Tertry	30/01/1918	06/03/1918
War Diary	Devise	13/03/1918	21/03/1918
War Diary	Viry	22/03/1918	23/03/1918

War Diary	Chauny	24/03/1918	25/03/1918
War Diary	Choisy-Au-Bac	27/03/1918	30/03/1918
Heading	6th Cav. Bde 3rd Cav. Div. War Diary 6th Machine Gun Squadron April 1918		
War Diary	E of Boves	01/04/1918	06/04/1918
War Diary	Camon	07/04/1918	30/04/1918
War Diary	Aumerval	30/04/1918	30/04/1918
War Diary	Contay	06/04/1918	16/04/1918
War Diary	Belloy	17/04/1918	30/04/1918
War Diary	Montigny	31/04/1918	13/06/1918
War Diary	Belloy	14/06/1918	24/06/1918
War Diary	Riencourt	25/06/1918	04/09/1918
War Diary	Le Mesge	05/09/1918	05/09/1918
War Diary	Petit St. Jean	06/09/1918	11/09/1918
War Diary	Riencourt	15/09/1918	21/09/1918
War Diary	Fieffs	22/09/1918	29/09/1918
War Diary	Grand Bouret	01/09/1918	05/09/1918
War Diary	Willeman	06/09/1918	18/09/1918
War Diary	Nuncq	19/09/1918	19/09/1918
War Diary	S"Leger	25/09/1918	25/09/1918
War Diary	Albert Area	26/09/1918	26/09/1918
War Diary	Hem	27/09/1918	27/09/1918
War Diary	Vermand	29/09/1918	31/09/1918
War Diary	Vermand Bellenglisle Vermand	01/10/1918	02/10/1918
War Diary	Bellenglisle Pontruet	03/10/1918	03/10/1918
War Diary	Trefcon G.30.c. U.12 5.7 B/49000	04/10/1918	09/10/1918
War Diary	P.23.d.	09/10/1918	09/10/1918
War Diary	Montigny	10/10/1918	10/10/1918
War Diary	Elincourt	11/10/1918	11/10/1918
War Diary	Banteux	13/10/1918	13/10/1918
War Diary	Etricourt	14/10/1918	14/10/1918
War Diary	Equancourt	23/10/1918	06/11/1918
War Diary	Sans-Lez-Marquion	06/11/1918	06/11/1918
War Diary	Esquerchin	07/11/1918	07/11/1918
War Diary	Peronne	08/11/1918	08/11/1918
War Diary	Vaulx-La-Tournai	10/11/1918	11/11/1918
War Diary	Bertincroix	13/11/1918	13/11/1918
War Diary	Fouleng	17/11/1918	17/11/1918
War Diary	Quenast	18/11/1918	18/11/1918
War Diary	Limelette	21/11/1918	21/11/1918
War Diary	Grand Rosiere	22/11/1918	22/11/1918
War Diary	Les Boscailles	24/11/1918	01/12/1918
War Diary	Leuze	10/12/1918	10/12/1918
War Diary	Fumal	12/12/1918	12/12/1918
War Diary	Yernawe	20/12/1918	20/12/1918
War Diary	Amay	08/01/1918	14/03/1918
War Diary	St. Georges	14/03/1919	30/04/1919
War Diary	Amay	01/05/1918	31/05/1918

(3)

WO 95/1152

3 Cavalry Division
6 Cavalry Brigade
6 Machine Gun Squadron

Feb. 1916 - May 1919.

1916-1919
3RD CAVALRY DIVISION
6TH CAVALRY BRIGADE.

6TH MACHINE GUN SQUADRON
FEB 1916-MAY 1919

WAR DIARY

Sheet I

INTELLIGENCE SUMMARY

6th Machine Gun Squadron

Feb. 1916 — May 1919

Army Form C. 2118

Place	Date	Hour	Summary of Events and Information	Remarks and references to Appendices
OFFIN (P&C)	29/2/1916		The Squadron was formed at OFFIN on the 29.2.16, and was composed as follows. Capt. G. Sartorius 6"B.C. (I.A.) in Command and 6 Subalterns. Capt G. SARTORIUS 6"B.C. AP LIEUT HOLT, LIEUT. HOPE (3rd Dragoon Guards) 2nd LIEUT J.B. BICKERSTETH, 2nd LIEUT A.R. COOPER (THE ROYAL DRAGOONS) 2nd LIEUT MOTISDALL (NORTH SOMERSET YEOMANRY) and 2nd LIEUT F.B. RATCLIFFE (THE ROYAL DRAGOONS, attached N.S.Y.) Other ranks 213 — two Sections of two guns each from the 3rd D.G's, I.R.D. + N.S.Y. — Each Section numbered A to F commanded by Subalterns in rank as above mentioned. The Squadron Sergeant Major + Farrier Sergeant were supplied by the R.D. and the Squadron Quartermaster Sergeant was supplied by the 3rd B.G. Armourer Sergeant attached from Ordnance. Total Horses 299. Each Section has had 3 limbers (ie each gun a limber and ammunition limber shared for 2 guns). Each section consists of one Subaltern one Sergeant and two Gun teams 2 in No: each Gun team 1 Gunner 3 pack ponies and one spare pack for looking and spare. Total strength Officers 7 N.C.O's men 311 Horses 47 Bicycle one (for Coste) The Squadron remained in permanent billets at OFFIN (P&C) from 29.2.16 to 1.5.16 and was occupied in preliminary Training and organization — Improving Packs — Cavalry action with 12 guns	

WAR DIARY or INTELLIGENCE SUMMARY

Place	Date	Hour	Summary of Events and Information	Remarks and references to Appendices
OFFIN	21/3/16		and drill, but work much hampered by enclosed character of country and wet weather. During this period leave to U.K. was in progress. G.O.C. 6th Cavalry Brigade inspected Squadron, the war & first turn out of the unit at full strength. The G.O.C. expressed his satisfaction and found by experience that it was impossible to work Squadron on establishment which was based on the absolute minimum. The G.O.C. was asked to increase the strength. This he did by attaching four men from each regiment in the brigade, thus bringing the strength up to 232.	
LE TOUQUET	1/5/16		The Squadron left OFFIN and moved into camp at LE TOUQUET where much useful work was done	

WAR DIARY or INTELLIGENCE SUMMARY

III Cavalry Division
6th M.G. Squadron
Vol 3
Army Form C. 2118.

May & June 1916.

Place	Date	Hour	Summary of Events and Information	Remarks and references to Appendices
LE TOUQUET	1/5/16	—	The Squadron proceeded to LE TOUQUET under Canvas. Normal routine – Sand dunes offered good opportunity for shooting. Useful indirect fire from hills above camp on to the shore.	
	10/5/16		Sports – mounted & dismounted – were held. Chief item interSquadron competition between Machine Gun & Hotchkiss. (6th I/Niskeomany)	
	15/5/16		Squadron proceeded to STRIQUIER for divisional training –	
	20/5/16		On the final I training proceeded back to former billets at OFFIN.	
	24/6/16		Squadron returned to LE TOUQUET from OFFIN – working as before	
	10/6/16		Squadron returned to billets – spent three days at TORCY.	
	15/6/16		Squadron proceeded to billets at CAURON-ST-MARTIN.	
	17/6/16		Capt Satorius handed over command of the Squadron temporarily to LIEUT. HOLT (3rd Dragoon Guards)	
	24/6/16		Squadron proceeded to DOMVAST by night –	
	25/6/16		Squadron continued night march to ST. LEGER-LE-DOMART.	
	26/6/16		Squadron left ST LEGER & arrived at BONNAY on morning of	

Army Form C. 2118.

WAR DIARY
or
INTELLIGENCE SUMMARY.

(Erase heading not required.)

 E.I.M.G. Squadron

Instructions regarding War Diaries and Intelligence Summaries are contained in F. S. Regs., Part II. and the Staff Manual respectively. Title pages will be prepared in manuscript.

Place	Date	Hour	Summary of Events and Information	Remarks and references to Appendices
BOMBAY.	27/6/16		of June 27th:-	
	30/6/16		Capt F. King (4th Hrs. and) assumed command of the Squadron.	JBB
	1/7/16			

Army Form C. 2118.

WAR DIARY
or
INTELLIGENCE SUMMARY.
(Erase heading not required.)

Instructions regarding War Diaries and Intelligence Summaries are contained in F. S. Regs., Part II. and the Staff Manual respectively. Title pages will be prepared in manuscript.

Place	Date	Hour	Summary of Events and Information	Remarks and references to Appendices
LE TOUQUET	27.6.16		The Squadron returned to billets and spent the days at TORCY. Squadron proceeded to billets at CAYRON-ST-MARTIN. Capt. Pritchard handed over command of the Squadron temporarily to Lieut. HOLT (3rd DRAGOON GUARDS). Squadron proceeded to DOMIAST by night. Squadron continued night march to 1st ST. LEGER-LE-DOMART. Squadron left ST LEGER & billeted at BONNAY on morning of JUNE 27th. CAPT. F. KING (15th HUSSARS) assumed command of the Squadron.	
	15.6.16			
	17.6.16			
	24.6.16			
	25.6.16			
	26.6.16			
	28.6.16			

F. King, Major,
Comdg. 15th H. Sqdn.

Army Form C. 2118.

WAR DIARY
or
INTELLIGENCE SUMMARY.
(Erase heading not required.)

6 a. M.G. Squadron.

Vol 5

Instructions regarding War Diaries and Intelligence Summaries are contained in F.S. Regs., Part II. and the Staff Manual respectively. Title pages will be prepared in manuscript.

Place	Date	Hour	Summary of Events and Information	Remarks and references to Appendices
BONNAY	1/7/16		Squadron "stood to" with rest of 3rd Cav: Div: hoping to go through the GAP. "Stood to" at 3 hrs notice for three days.	
	4/7/16		Squadron moved back to WIRY-AU-MONT (W. of AIRAINES) & stayed there till when it moved to CORBIE.	
	9/7/16			
	10/7/16		Squadron with 6th Cav: BDE: proceeded to VAUX-SUR-SOMME where it remained under canvas till	
	20/7/16		when it moved to LA NEUVILLE	
	29/7/16		Received orders to be up to 3rd Corps area to construct and garrison strong points in second line. O.C. 3 subalterns 12 guns & 6 gun numbers & Gun proceeded with Limbers to BECOURT.	
	30/7/16		Party went to N.W. corner of MAMETZ WOOD. From there limbers were sent back. Three strong points occupied. Royals Section (4 guns) occupied point in road at N.W. corner of MAMETZ WOOD - 3rd D.G. Section (4 guns) occupied strong point at N.E corner of MAMETZ WOOD. MSY Section (4 guns) occupied strong point 100 yards S. of N.W. corner of BAZENTIN LE PETIT wood. None of these strong points had been constructed, and as	

Army Form C. 2118.

WAR DIARY
or
INTELLIGENCE SUMMARY.
(Erase heading not required.)

8th M.G. Squadron.

Place	Date	Hour	Summary of Events and Information	Remarks and references to Appendices
			Shell fire (shrapnel & high explosive) was pretty heavy & continuous the action had to get the horses(?) under cover as soon as they could. Shell fire from 9 p.m. till midnight very heavy, but very few casualties.	
	31/7/16		Owing to withdrawal of 3rd Cav: Div: from the 4th Army area, M.G. detachments ordered to hand over stirrup pumps & return to 2A NEUVILLE	

JBB

Army Form C. 2118.

WAR DIARY
or
INTELLIGENCE SUMMARY. 6 Machine Gun Sqn. Sheet 7.

Vol 6

Place	Date	Hour	Summary of Events and Information	Remarks and references to Appendices
LA NEUVILLE	1/8/16		The Brigade moved to CADOUS, billets there nights 1/2 & 2/3rd & on the 3rd inst moved to MAINTENAY and continued the march on the 4th inst to permanent billets at CAVRON ST MARTIN	
CAVRON ST MARTIN	5/8/16 to 26/8/16		The daily routine Training & permanent billets looked from 5/8/16 to 26/8/16 during which the Squadron in sections in Gun Drill, Musketeers & Firing — several good short ranges having been found close to billets — One team per section visited the R.H.A. at HUMBERCOURT daily for instruction in driving — sections also took part in small tactical schemes sends. 2nd Lieut W.H. GREEN (12 Reserve Regt of Cavalry) and 2nd Lieut G.H. EATON (19th Hussars) joined the Squadron from the M.G. Base Depot.	
	23/8/16		The Squadron received orders that the Brigade moves fortnite march EAST on Friday the 25th inst.	ADL

WAR DIARY
or
INTELLIGENCE SUMMARY.

Army Form C. 2118.

6 M.G. Squadron Sheet 8

Place	Date	Hour	Summary of Events and Information	Remarks and references to Appendices
CAYEN	25/8/16		The order re the Brigade marching EAST was cancelled, & the Squadron received orders to hold themselves in readiness to proceed to the II Corps to relieve the 8th M.G. Sqn who are holding strong points around THIEPVAL.	
	27/8/16		The C.O., 6 Officers & 94 O.R. with 12 guns left by Motor lorries to the II Corps.	
	27/8/16 to 3/9/16		The lorries and the remainder of the Sqn, 2 Officers, 152 O.R., remained at CARNOY ST MARTIN.	
	3/9/16		2nd W.P. CLOWES (8 troopers) joined the Squadron on 30/8/16	

2nd W.P. Clowes

Army Form C. 2118.

WAR DIARY
or
INTELLIGENCE SUMMARY.

C Sqdn. M.G. Squadron Sheet 9.

(Erase heading not required.)

Vol 7

Instructions regarding War Diaries and Intelligence Summaries are contained in F.S. Regs., Part II. and the Staff Manual respectively. Title pages will be prepared in manuscript.

Place	Date	Hour	Summary of Events and Information	Remarks and references to Appendices
BEAUMONT HAMEL – THIEPVAL	3/9/16		Squadron took part in an attack on THIEPVAL. 4 (Royals) guns in line opp: THIEPVAL. 4 (3rd D Gs) guns on ridge behind HAMEL. 4 (N8Y) guns in reserve in AVELUY WOOD. Guns went into these positions on Aug 30. Zero time for attack was 5.10 a.m. Attack failed – in most cases Machine Gunners had to retire behind the infantry. Apparently no reason unless viewed by Germans, despised on English officers which happened on one or two occasions. Squadron only had 4 Casualties (shell shock).	
	4/9/16		Squadron relieved after five days in the trenches.	
	6/9/16		N8Y guns went up to HAMEL ridge took over positions before occupied by 3rd DG guns. They had fine time there only then orders were received to concentrate guns at BOUZINCOURT with a view to returning to CAYRON.	
	7/9/16		Squadron returned by night lorry to CAYRON.	
	8/9/16		Given 48 hours to prepare for cavalry move – everything has to be transferred from M.G. Infantry to Cavalry basis.	
	10/9/16		Squadron moved with Brigade en route for the SOMME. Billeted at STUCHOY in the AUTHIE valley.	

N.B. 5/9/16 2/Lt. F.B. RATCLIFFE left Sqdn for ENGLAND where he reported at Instructor at TIDWORTH.

WAR DIARY or INTELLIGENCE SUMMARY.

Army Form C. 2118.

Sir M. G. Sqdn. Sheet 10.

Place	Date	Hour	Summary of Events and Information	Remarks and references to Appendices
	11/9/16		Bde moved to new area — Squadron billeting at NEUILLY L'HÔPITAL	
	12/9/16		Bde moved to LA CHAUSSÉE. Squadron at TIRANCOURT CHATEAU with Bde HQrs.	
	14/9/16		Bde camped at BUSSY — the rest of the Division being near by. Concentration of the Cavalry division in SOMME area —	
	15/9/16		1/3 Bde camped a few hundred yards W. of BONNAY. Great attack on the GUEUDECOURT—MORVAL line begun. Into the 3rd Cav: Div: Camped along the HALLUE river W. of DAOURS — PONT-NOYELLES road.	
	17/9/16		Much rain — Camp, situated on stubble field, in indescribable state. 24 Clones (8 Knows) allowed to transfer from the Sqdn to their own regiment.	
	22/9/16		Divison began to move back. Bde occupied LEMERGE — SOUES area. Sqdn being billeted at latter place.	
	23/9/16		Bde moved North to BEAUCOURT — HAVANS area. Sqdn billeted BEAUCOURT.	
	24/9/16		Sqdn billeted at ROUSSENT — Bde area very scattered, running from MAINTENAY in N.W. Inclus. as far as MERLIMONT	

T2134. Wt. W708—776. 500000. 4/15. Sir J.C. & S.

WAR DIARY
or
INTELLIGENCE SUMMARY. 6/2 M.G. Sqdn. Sheet 11

Army Form C. 2118.

Vol #8

Place	Date	Hour	Summary of Events and Information	Remarks and references to Appendices
	24/9/16 – 20/10/16		Squadron billeted at ROUSSENT. Horses still in fields. Men & OR's under cover. Time occupied in small "schemes" with the regiments of 6/15 Brigade and in modern classes etc.	
	21/10/16		Squadron went into winter billets at VERTON. 2/Lt A.R. Cooper proceeded to England & reported at UCKFIELD as instructor at 1st Reserve M.G. Cavalry Regiment for six weeks.	
	21/10/16		2/Lt R.A. SPONG joined the Squadron.	
	21/10/16 – 31/10/16		Time occupied in improving stabling & in getting settled into permanent winter billets. Except for Brigade HQ's Squadron had village to itself and in a few days good stabling was found for the 300 horses. A good deal of work had however to be done to improve standings. Chalk & cinders were hauled from MERLIMONT & RANG DU FLIERS for this purpose.	

JRB

JB Ratcliff Kent
Comdt 6 M.G. Sqdn

WAR DIARY
INTELLIGENCE SUMMARY. 6. H.G.S.R. Sheet 12.
NOVEMBER

Vol 9

Place	Date	Hour	Summary of Events and Information	Remarks and references to Appendices
VERTON	11/16		Having more or less settled down into lines the Sqn. continues its training. Sections went daily to the Sands to practise small advances attacks and men were taught how to get guns quickly off their feet: Twice a week sections paraded at Rifting School — a large field at the end of the village — in which 6 jumps have been built — There are horses jumped untimed — 2 previously the letter — Park, horse harness rapidly untimed and these too can be untimed rapidly — has also begun and teams too for 3 Dragoon gs took part — Sections details were on duty both Cussing scheme — all the shell French Cussing scheme — lies central — Inexpensible rides for gun numbers has instituted — During the month Lt. TISDALL, Sgt. HARDING went through an 'Anti Gas Course' at the Div. Gas School. General Leave re-opened this month	[signature]

WAR DIARY
or
INTELLIGENCE SUMMARY.

Army Form C. 2118.

Place	Date	Hour	Summary of Events and Information	Remarks and references to Appendices
VERTON	1/12/16		Lt BICKERSTETH Sgt CORNISH Cpl WITTENBACH proceeded to England on duty as instructors at Machine Gun Training Centre at UCKFIELD.	

Army Form C. 2118.

WAR DIARY
or
INTELLIGENCE SUMMARY

5th Machine Gun Squadron Sheet 123

DECEMBER Vol 10

Place	Date	Hour	Summary of Events and Information	Remarks and references to Appendices
VERTON	1/12/16		2 Bucksatch Sgt Cornick Cpl Witterford proceeded to England for duty as instructors at Machine Gun Training Centre, UCKFIELD.	
	17/12/16 – 22/12/16		H Cooper & Sgt Twist returned from UCKFIELD 17-11-16. Parades as usual. Seeing went to Ruling School twice a week and on the Sands the Remainder	
MARESQUEL	22/12/16		The Sqdn. moved from billets at MARESQUEL on ECQUEMICOURT. H.Q and A.D.P. & Sections in the former. B,C,&E Sections and E.C.B section in the latter. billets at Ecquemicourt very bad and horses suffered a great deal from the change from last billets where they were well housed.	
VERTON	11/12/16		Inspection full strength marching order by G.O.C. 3rd Cav. Div. Sqdn was seen in Riding, Discipline and	J M ? chain

Army Form C. 2118.

WAR DIARY
or
INTELLIGENCE SUMMARY. [Signed] J McManus Comm[anding] Squadron
Sheet 114

DECEMBER 1916 (Erase heading not required.)

Instructions regarding War Diaries and Intelligence Summaries are contained in F. S. Regs., Part II. and the Staff Manual respectively. Title pages will be prepared in manuscript.

Place	Date	Hour	Summary of Events and Information	Remarks and references to Appendices
VERTON	14/12/16		a Tactical Scheme involving (1) Crossing a Head line - Employment of 12 guns to support an attack against BAHOT WOOD by 2 minutes attack on Left and dismounted attack on the Right. O.C. expressed himself extremely pleased with the Sqd[ron]s Effort was made to carry out a field day scheme on the Sands but owing to the departure of Riflemen "B" G.O.S. was unable Scheme.	
			Tiffney Promotion took place 2nd Lieut J B BICKERSTETH } app[ointed] Temp[orary] Lieutenant 1/10/1916 A R COOPER C H ELMES Temp Lt J B Ratcliffe app[ointe]d Acting Captain 15/11/1916	16/11/1916 29/28/1916 2/5 21/12/1916
MARESQUEL				

WAR DIARY
INTELLIGENCE SUMMARY

DECEMBER 1916

Place: MARESQUEL

Lt C.H. FLMES seconded to M.G. Corps. 7/12/16
29 dates 18/12/1916

Lt R.S. LONG proceeded to England 29/12/1916 to finish his structure qualify as a Dental Surgeon — for two months —

The Sgt — every to the move of Billetts two days before being confirmed did not leave any day but a dinner was arranged to see the New Year in —

Army Form C. 2118.

WAR DIARY
or
INTELLIGENCE SUMMARY.   6th M.G. Sqdn.
(Erase heading not required.)

JANUARY 1917   Sheet 16

Place	Date	Hour	Summary of Events and Information	Remarks and references to Appendices
MAREQUEL ECQUENICOURT	1/1/17		The first fortnight of this year was almost exclusively spent in improving stabling - or more strictly in creating it - as the squadron has never been worse off. It is also the first time the squadron has been divided up in two villages and its arrangement is very unsatisfactory from every point of view. Horses were kept fit & hard by Route marches. Rain was very continuous till about the 20th & then cold weather with extremely hard frost set in.	
	22/1/17		Lt W.H. Green proceeded to England for duty as instructor at MACHINE GUN (CAVALRY) TRAINING CENTRE at UCKFIELD.	
	26/1/17		Lt J.B. Bickersteth returned from UCKFIELD.	
	30/1/17		Five officers & eighty-seven other ranks proceeded to trenches - (Officers Major King, Capt Ratcliffe, Lts Tisdall, Cooper, Eaton) Squn in position W. of VIMY RIDGE near main ARRAS-SOUCHEZ road. VILLERS-AU-BOIS neat billet & motor lorries took the party from MAREQUIL to the village.	

T2134. Wt. W708-776. 500000. 4/15. Sir J.C. & S.

WAR DIARY or INTELLIGENCE SUMMARY

Army Form C. 2118.

12th 19[..] J.G.S. Sheet 7

Vol 12

Place	Date	Hour	Summary of Events and Information	Remarks and references to Appendices
SOUCHEZ	12th		Sqn. The Squadron designated with 8 Y.O.R. and 5 officers. Left Marœuil for SOUCHEZ for attachment to 4th Canadian Div. Guns were in position along from SOUCHEZ - ARRAS road in groups of 4 guns, attached to machine gun emphacements of H.Q. in 8th Canadian Inf. Bde. Guns were used extensively for shelting indirect on enemy's ration parties and dumps at SH- GIVENCHY VILLAGE - Qa, cone of attack and group of gun& had an S.O.S. target - During first 10 days guns took part in many raids and supplied a box barrage.	
	13th		Sqn. had allotted and took up a position 900 × 3 of SOUCHEZ Village overlooking ZOUAVE VALLEY and prepared positions for 8 of the 12 guns. The Sqn. was ordered to be ready to move by night of 15/16th to cooperate in a large raid which was	main

J.G.[signature]

WAR DIARY
INTELLIGENCE SUMMARY.

Army Form C. 2118.

July — 4 M.G.C. Sheet. 18.

Place	Date	Hour	Summary of Events and Information	Remarks and references to Appendices
SOUCHEZ	14/7/17 15/7		Shorter to Gbby Avenue — gas was to be used on a large scale. 8 guns were in position — It guns in reserve. As day cut (gas fire) along the main road — 50 yards from gun posture. The Canadian Div. attacked at 3 am — the wind however right for the first time in 10 days. Barrage fire a enemy's mil flash has fixed by the Sqd. for 2½ hrs during which time 67000 rds were expended — 40 guns (M.G.) were in action. Total expenditure from 5.40.00 rds —	
VILLIERS Bois	13/7		Sqdt. was in Hdavon from here and ordered to get ready to embark on the 23rd	
MARANT	23/7		Returned to HARESQUEL arriving there — no casualties. Rod. has sustained during the march —	
"	15/7		No 50501 SQMS SUTTON H.C. M.G.C. No. 50501 SQMS SUTTON H.C. [?] MILITARY No 50533 Pte [?] Pte D.Dec H.Q. A.91. MEDAL	
"	16/7		a/t C.Q. LOWDEN James Sgt. for duty posted to B Section. MEDAILLE MILITAIRE	

f. M[signature]

WAR DIARY
INTELLIGENCE SUMMARY

Army Form C. 2118

6 M.G. Sqⁿ

March 1917

Sheet 19

Place	Date	Hour	Summary of Events and Information	Remarks and references to Appendices
MUNICIPAL CABARET ROUGE	1/3/17		Alberta Sqⁿ was relieved in the trenches on VIMY RIDGE and returned to rest billets at VILLERS AU BOIS –	
MAREQUE	2/3/17		Sqⁿ returned in horse lines from the line –	
"	3/3/17 – 10/3/17		This week was spent in getting the horses right again after 1 months stay in the trenches and in seeing to all the issues B.F.g. – Seating stated a dismounted training preparatory to being possibly from the April. – There were inspections + then were glad to get a little Hun hung-mounted harness in the mornings – and field exercises Recognizance of an afternoon	
	11/3/17 – 13/3/17		In men + in horses have learned out to farmers at HERMOND to	
	13/3/17		help their plough –	
	26/3/17		Horses returned from ploughing – in all a few cases too they fallen away	
	27/3/17		En route March from to trucks – stated in a Brigade – Sqⁿ was congratulated on condition of its horses on return out by G.O.C. 3ᵈ Cav. Dv.	
	31/3/17		JR.A. Shaly Stuck off. J/ony hayln	

WAR DIARY

Army Form C. 2118

INTELLIGENCE SUMMARY

C.M.G.S. Sheet 20.
April 1917. Vol 14

Place	Date	Hour	Summary of Events and Information	Remarks and references to Appendices
MARESQUEL	4/17		Sqd. was preparing to leave MARESQUEL, all spare stores were being sent away + huts struck. Orders were received for 3 Sections and B.H.Q. to move down to ECQUEMICOURT as the 5th & 8th Bns. were being concentrated in huts - preparatory to moving in direction of ARRAS.	
	5/17		Sqd. at ECQUEMICOURT, huts in a large field on roadside - rear manure cover in camp.	
VACQUERIE	7/17		Bn. marched East to billets about VACQUERIE - Sqd. was in a nice Chateau field at FORTEL in Commune of VACQUERIE	
FOSSEUX	8/17		Bn. Continues its march and Sqd. was billetted at FOSSEUX - men in huts a kilometre away from horses -	
ARRAS	9/17		Bn. moved up behind 8th Bn. and took its head on Cav. track in ARRAS about 8 pm. Sqd. was ordered to Halt where it stood on road - found excellent shelter and all ranks + men were comfortable and asleep by 9:30 p.m. Message was received at 11 p.m. ordering Sqd. to be ready to move back	

WAR DIARY
or INTELLIGENCE SUMMARY

Army Form C. 2118

April 6th G.S. Sheet 21

Place	Date	Hour	Summary of Events and Information	Remarks and references to Appendices
DUISANS and ARRAS	10/4/17		At 7 hours time - Sqn: was ready and had Bn. back to a field near DUISANS. Bde left DUISANS again about 11 AM and moved up on cavalry track. One Bn. troop up a portion of trenches in FEUCHY VALLEY - Sqn. was close by the valley road but owing to systematic searching by the enemy with H.E. moved back both east of Bn. about to shell -	
ARRAS	11/4/17		About 6 a.m. Sqn. was ready for action as it had been decided to move forward for the "gap" - in the operations the following sections of Cav. G.S. were employed B: F: F: D. and their experiences in relation below —	
ARRAS	11/4/17		At 8:30 am B section which had already been detailed for duty with 3rd D.G. moved forward with B Sqn 3 D.G.s (Captain Hughes-Smith) and took up a position on ridge E of road running from LA BERGERE to MONCHY Section had a good	H. Hughes

WAR DIARY or INTELLIGENCE SUMMARY

Army Form C. 2118.

Month: April   6th G.S.   Sheet 22

Place	Date	Hour	Summary of Events and Information	Remarks and references to Appendices

ARRAS

Held off fire - Section Posts from Right range of Mill 100 - Sir ROBERT
Fortes - numerous shots of Recess were engaged & dispersed -
At 11:30 A.M. Lt. LOWDEN Cmdg. A. Section was wounded by an
17 Pr. enemy Shell burst at the Junction - Sgt. EATON Hen a 2nd in
Command and took very Officer came over & 9 am position & his great
And able Assistants. He relieved Sgt. Lafferty at 11:30 A.M.
Casualties 1 Officer and 1 man wounded -
At 8 P.M. 9 an. German Officer Major Philip, to take "A" Section
wanted to Surrender, Cpl. Byrd who was in command of the
Post - D. Section Wedny Lt. COOPER's mountebank but came
over when Wedny brought fire for from QUENAPE and let 5 Inch
have (single drum the) officer surrender. Section was much
alarmed and F Section here rushed three rifles & grenade -
at 4 P.M. F Section Advanced by E Section commanded later - He
forces under Lt. EMMS - the Actg. Cmdr. Lt. TISDAIL appeared
to be a demented half from M.G.y bullet all Sutton

WAR DIARY

Army Form C. 2118

Sheet 28/23

INTELLIGENCE SUMMARY — Chas.

Place: Ahe

Date	Hour	Summary of Events and Information
10/4/17		Patrols for 24 BERGER— These Sections found 3 guns in the line and one in reserve and manned the ridge East of the sunken road leading from there to Guemappe, a further party patrols Hurley and German were exposed. 2 Counter attacks has already been launched, and a third was expected — Heavy shells all the time. These 2 Section has only 3 men killed and 3 wounded, and have returned at 11:30pm. Snow storms + Hypanis had been the order of the day and weather was the worst experienced for 3 years — men and especially horses suffered considerably.
	At 12.30 a.m.	Sqn has collected about to its strength muster heard King (the Regiment had made their own way in) left
		thereby in mask for RACE-COURSE outside ARRAS. Orders to go via Cavalry Track which found impassable. So had by them road to ARRAS — a biting cold wind and J Kingham

WAR DIARY or INTELLIGENCE SUMMARY — Bdes.

Army Form C. 2118
Sheet 24

April

Place	Date	Hour	Summary of Events and Information	Remarks and references to Appendices
FOSSEUX	12/4/17		Heavy Platts manoeuvres – Men and horses very tired and men were asleep in their saddles – Brigade all the time – readies manoeuvre at 5:30 am or rather its neighbourhoods manoeuvre could not to find because Brigade flotted anything out – So tied up anywhere – men fell asleep for 1½ hr in a barn – packed very flesh – at 4.0 am gave him a large corn feed and got ready to move at 9.0 am – Bde. moves as a Bde. to FOSSEUX where it remains for four days.	
VAULX	16/4/17		Bde. moves West to Manouevrens area West of AVn-le-CHATEAU. Sqn. billetted in VAULX – wonderful accommodation stayed here 3 days. visited by G.O.C. 3 Cav. Dm. – Speech to men. –	
VAULX	20/4/17		Sqn. found out permanent billets at BUIRE-LE-SEC. Very good accommodation water doubtful –	J. Markham

WAR DIARY
or
INTELLIGENCE SUMMARY

Army Form C. 2118

(Erase heading not required.)

April (Aug. S. Sheet 25)

Place	Date	Hour	Summary of Events and Information	Remarks and references to Appendices
BUIRE-LE-SEC	20th-30th		Days spent in refitting and getting horses shod up and trimmed. Wounds seem to... Horses receive very little, but grazing every day. Forage in abundance and more than ever available. S.O.C. orders horses no work but to be allowed to graze and get fit again.	
	3/17		*) L. WILKES, M.C.C. (Lowest Sgt.) had been invalided home from SAUI-CULI-Ath charge of Sgt. dismounted party 17 in number as 1st Reinforcement.	
	25th		*) Lt. ELLIS M.C.C. Joins as Sgt.	
			Total Casualties in Sqn.	
			2 Officers (wounded) 3 men (killed) 3 men (wounded)	
			Lt A R COOPER	
			Lt C G LOWDEN	
			36 horses killed + wounded	J.C.—[signature]

1875 Wt. W503/826 1,000,000 4/15 J.B.C.& A. A.D.S.S./Forms/C. 2118.

Army Form C. 2118

May 192[?] 6th Machine Gun Sqn. Sheet 26

WAR DIARY
INTELLIGENCE SUMMARY
(Erase heading not required.)

Vol 15

Place	Date	Hour	Summary of Events and Information	Remarks and references to Appendices
BUIRE-LE-SEC	1/5/17	11.5/17	Sqn. was employed in Training. The batch of Remounts which had recently been issued from the Base-Remaking classes were held daily. Units of BS also sent men to be instructed - O.C. the remounts vicinity of BUIRE consists of long dry valleys and rough ravines cut into them - advantage was taken of these as ranges and much good musketry work was put in by every troop every afternoon.	
	2/5/17		45 NCO's and men arrived as a permanent dismounted party raising Sqn. establishment up to 55 OR.	
	5/17 18/17	5 7	Sqn. marched by easy stages from fleets to Picrones at BUIRE NE of PERONNE passing through the following places, and staying night	
	10	13	RAYE SUR - AUTHIE	
	11	14	BARLY — one day	
	13	14	PERNOIS — one day	
	14		BUSSY — midday	
	15/16		HARBONIERES — one day	
	17/18/19		BUIRE — two days	
	19		At BUIRE a permanent camp was made	JK

Army Form C. 2118

64 Machine Gun Sqn - Sheet 27

WAR DIARY
or
INTELLIGENCE SUMMARY
(Erase heading not required.)

Place	Date	Hour	Summary of Events and Information	Remarks and references to Appendices
Buire	May 29/30	1a.a.	All ranks moved up to EPEHY with 10 guns to take up a line of trenches N.E. of the Village – Sqn. took over gun positions of 3rd Machine Gun Sqn. in Subsection D. of D. Sector. The boundaries of the latter being from TOMBOIS FM (excl.) to TANGIBLE RAVINE (incl.) by the former, TOMBOIS FM (excl.) to CATELET COPSE (incl.). Sqn. have disposed as follows:— 2 guns in the BIRDCAGE (S. of OSSUS W.) Outpost line. 7 guns in the Intermediate or Green Line. 8 guns in the Brown Line. All the guns were well placed and had excellent cross fire. Anti aircraft guns. [Offr.] was detailed each pair of guns and came under the orders of the Subsection Comm. either through the Commanders of the Intermediate section of defence in which guns were—or through Sqn. leader when HQ was at No 13 Cpoa at HQ of &c. D. Subsection – There had a very quick time. 3 lines of fire were laid out for each gun in Green and Outpost Lines —	JR

WAR DIARY or INTELLIGENCE SUMMARY

Army Form C. 2118

(Erase heading not required.)

Place	Date	Hour	Summary of Events and Information	Remarks and references to Appendices
FREHY	29/5		S.O.S. line for defence of Outpost line commands, aeroplane flares, shooting flyers all their communications, aeroplane etc. Transport of 6 limbers here used for transporting etc every evening up to Sept 19 — waggon lines being at VILLERS FAUCON. Sqn was served it would do nine days in the line and nine days out followed by 18 days in and 18 days out - No casualties of any description occurred during tour of duty and only one man reported sick. Captain J.B. RATCLIFFE remained behind in camp i/c Details.	

J.B. Ratcliffe

Army Form C. 2118

Sheet 29

WAR DIARY
INTELLIGENCE SUMMARY

June 6th 9 S.

Place	Date	Hour	Summary of Events and Information	Remarks and references to Appendices
BUIRE	2/6/17	—	Lt. J.A. GUTHRIE M.G.C. joined this Sqn. Mentioned in Despatches. No 50537 S.S.M. WALTER J. L.G. 29 5/17	
"	3/6/17 – 8/6/17		Riding School for Recruits and latest recruits. Remainder of Sqn kept grazing for 2 hours daily. Lectures for all gun numbers every afternoon. Also instruction in use of LEWIS + GERMAN GUNS. also GERMAN bombs	
	9/10 June		Sqn. proceeded to the Trenches and took over defence of D2 Subsector - under the command of Captain J.B. RATCLIFFE. 9 guns were disposed for defence of Germany line with 2 guns in Outpost line and 1 on anti-aircraft duty in second line	
	11th June		2nd Lieut J. KING. took over duties of D.M.G.O. and entrusted the 2h guns in D Sector.	
	10th June		2 Horses were killed by lightning + 2 men badly hurt.	

J. King

Army Form C. 2118

WAR DIARY
or
INTELLIGENCE SUMMARY

6... G.S.

June 1917

Vol 16 Stat 30

Place	Date	Hour	Summary of Events and Information	Remarks and references to Appendices
EPEHY	1st June to 28th June		Sqn. was disposed in Dr. Sulcecto for defence of Intermediate Line. Indirect fire was carried out against German trains/dumps as well as station lights in VENDHUILE - the latter with some success. The Sqn. also supplied a boy lennage for two bases in German trenches - nothing of further importance resumed. L. J. B. Buchanan KH was lranss to 1st ROYAL DRAGOONS to take charge of two Hotchkiss Rifles detailed during the said to engage German machine gun.	
	June 28th		Sqn. was humedly withdrawn from the line as ordered the ready to hand mounts on July 3rd.	

J.C.M. Major

WAR DIARY or INTELLIGENCE SUMMARY

Army Form C. 2118

July 1917   6 M.G.C.   Sheet 31

Place	Date	Hour	Summary of Events and Information	Remarks and references to Appendices
BUIRE	July 1st		Sqn. was preparing to move North - mounted	
	July 2nd			
	July 3rd		Sqn. started its march by easy stages to AUCHEL, staying one night at each of following places. SUZANNE - MERICOURT - ANPLIER ETRÉE WAMIN AMMURY. AUCHEL July 9th.	
AUCHEL	July 9th		Sqn. was billeted in AUCHEL & Sqn. in a field east of church and other ½ in a smaller field the west of church - Owing to the distance which Sqn. had to go daily for water (2 miles) the days were no long stable hour. For these 10 days Section practised coming in and out of action from new packs -	
	July 17th		Sqn. marched to present billets at LE TOUQUET. in HAVERSKERQUE area.	
LE TOUQUET	July 18th / July 31st		Routine consists of stables - mechanism - dismounted training was possible owing to high state of cultivation. G.O.C. 6 C.B. inspects Sqn. full marching order. Lt A COLE M.G.C. joined Sqn. from M.G. Base. Mens leave was offered the Sqn. than it could accept consistent with it remaining ready for immediate action.	

J Mag/Major
6 M.G.C

Army Form C. 2118

WAR DIARY
or
INTELLIGENCE SUMMARY
(Erase heading not required.)

6 M.G. Sqdn
Sheet 3
August 1917 Vol 18

Place	Date	Hour	Summary of Events and Information	Remarks and references to Appendices
LE TOUQUET	1/8/17		The Squadron remained in billets, time was occupied in training. Leave was continued and the Squadron was able to send all men on leave to U.K. with 18 months (or over) service in France.	
	16/8/17		Inspection by the Corps Machine Gun Officer. The Squadron was represented in various events in Brigade Divisional & Corps horse shows. Major J.F. King went to Camiers M.G. School	
	31/8/17		on one months advanced M.G. Barrage fire. During the month very bad weather was experienced, the lines had to be continually moved from standings in fields to roads in the vicinity.	

J.B.Ratcliffe (Capt)

Army Form C. 2118

WAR DIARY
or
INTELLIGENCE SUMMARY
(Erase heading not required.)

6ᵗʰ Machine Gun Squadron Sheet 33

September 1917

Vol 19

Place	Date	Hour	Summary of Events and Information	Remarks and references to Appendices
LE TOUQUET	1st		The C.O. Major J. King was absent all this month undergoing a course of advanced M.G. training, consequently devolved a Barrage work. The command devolved on the 2nd in Command, Capt. J. B. Ratcliffe. The time was occupied in training. Riding School for Officers, N.C.O.s & men - Pack lines - Remounts, frequent schemes took place both Brigade and Regimental, in which the Squadron, sometimes as a unit and sometimes with subsections, took part. Time was found for several Horse Show & Sports meetings which were very successful - Leave to England still continued with the result that all men who had over 15 months in the Country were able to get leave. Major J. King resumed Command of the Squadron on the 30th	
"	30			J B Ratcliffe Capt
M Clarke Capt

WAR DIARY
INTELLIGENCE SUMMARY

6a M.G. Sqn. Oct. 1917 Sheet 34

Vol 20

Place	Date	Hour	Summary of Events and Information	Remarks and references to Appendices
HAVERSKERQUE (LE TOUQUET)	15/10/17 - 10/10/17		Sqn. was employed in training/pack horses + subsection work in the mornings and in the afternoon. Gun pits were practised in the new Barrage Drill. It having been decided to employ Vickers guns in lifts of 8 guns in future - Sqn. took part in several schemes with Regt. S. of ST. VENANT.	
	18/10/17		On 17th orders were rec'd to move S. next day. Sqn left for billets in ABBEVILLE area staying 3 nights at BOTAVAL - one night at BONNIÈRES arriving in new area on 24th & Sqn. being disposed as follows H.Q + 4 Subsections in EPAGNE + 2 Subsections in EAGNETTE - men + horses very comfortable.	
	24/10/17			
	24/10/17 - 31/10/17		Training was suspended for a week men were given a chance to clean up + improve billets.	
	26/10/17		1st S.G. HIBBERT. M.G.C. reported for duty.	
	29/10/17		2nd T. ELLIS + 27 O.R. left as a digging party for DOINGT - Lt. T. A. GUTHRIE to England sick struck off	

J. Vaughan
Major

WAR DIARY of 6th M.G. Squadron

INTELLIGENCE SUMMARY

November 1917 Vol Sheet 21

Place	Date	Hour	Summary of Events and Information	Remarks and references to Appendices
EPAGNE	1/11/17 to 17/11/17		Squadron remained in billets and was exercised in M.G. & rifle shooting – mounted – Mounter M.G. work. Bare horsemen. Remounts were given further instruction – all Squadron football was organised by the Brigade. One Officer (Capt Ratcliffe) and one Sergeant (Sgt Hamnett) proceeded to Small Arms School G.H.Q. for advanced training in M.G. Barrage fire.	
	17/11/17 18/11/17		The Brigade moved east. The Squadron billets at BEAUCOURT on the 18th at Susanne where with the remainder of the Division they remained in reserve to the 3rd Army during the battle of CAMBRAI, and on the 23rd moved back to	
RUBEMPRÉ.	23/11/17 28/11/17			
	30/11/17		The Squadron comprises 2 8 guns, AB D & F sub sections, 5 Officers 99 O.R. were warned to prepare for trenches with the dismounted Battalion formed by the Brigade and were ordered to proceed next day to by two The Trench party there ordered to proceed next day to by two to the seats allotted to the Brigade.	FB Ratcliffe Capt 6 M.G. Sqn

Army Form C. 2118

6th Machine Gun Squadron

(SHEET 37)

Vol 2.2

WAR DIARY
or
INTELLIGENCE SUMMARY
(Erase heading not required.)

December 1917

Place	Date	Hour	Summary of Events and Information	Remarks and references to Appendices
RUBEMPRÉ	1/12/17 – 21/12/17		Horses and remainder of Sqdn stayed in billets at RUBEMPRÉ	
	21/12/17		Squadron (less dismounted party) marched back to old billets at ÉPAGNE-ÉPAGNETTE. Owing to snow, this march was carried out under very difficult conditions, the Squadron not arriving in billets till 11.30. pm.	
	9/12/17		While at RUBEMPRÉ Squadron sent away 19 horses to MARSEILLES and thence to EGYPT.	
	4/12/17		LT A B TODD reported for duty.	

M. Ashwith Lt

WAR DIARY
INTELLIGENCE SUMMARY

Army Form C. 2118

6th Machine Gun Sqn.

Sheet 36

Place	Date	Hour	Summary of Events and Information	Remarks and references to Appendices
RUBEMPRÉ	1/12/17		Major King & Officers & 77 O.R. proceeded by bus to HANCOURT and billeted there three nights.	
	5/12/17		Took over MG positions - only 8 guns were taken up from 7th MG Sqn. Two sections took over gun position in Chateau & BOIS DE PRIEL. The remaining four guns occupied its post at TEMPLEUX and RONSOY.	
	8/12/17			
	10/12/17		LE VERGUIER. Subsequently two guns heretofore at FAGOT COPSE and two guns were brought from its Chateau to LE VERGUIER. Guns remained in these positions to end of the month. Major F. King performed Duties of B.M.Go for the first ten days and then assumed command of all the guns of the dismounted division.	
	8/12/17		LT ELMES took over command of the Squadron guns from LT EATON.	
	31/12/17		Major King handed over Command to Major Chomley (7th MG Sqn) and the following day proceeded to England to report to GRANTHAM, upon this date ceased to command 6th MG Sqn.	

JA Chomley Lt

WAR DIARY or INTELLIGENCE SUMMARY

Army Form C. 2118

6 M.G. Squadron

January 1918 — Sheet 38

Place	Date	Hour	Summary of Events and Information	Remarks and references to Appendices
EPAGNE	2/1/18		Two officers (Lieut Hibbert & Lieut TODD) and 2 O.R. & Carriers proceeded to a relief with French Party. Lieuts Elmes & EATON with 20 O.R. relieved from trenches 4/1/18	
	3/1/18		Major F. King awarded the D.S.O. — L.G. M. 2/1/18	
	4/1/18		Major F. King D.S.O. to England } Struck off strength Lieut C.H. ELMES to Tank Corps } 2/Lt C.C. Smith arrived from Base & is taken on strength Capt Sim O the Squadron Commanded by Lieut Ole remained in battle positions in and about le VERGUIER until the night of 14/15th when they were relieved by the 2nd M.G. Squadron — They rejoined the remainder of the Squadron at EPAGNE on the 15th Strength 5 Officers 91 O.R.	
	16		Casualties Nº 51327 Cpl Coxall } Killed in action 3/1/1/18 Nº 51792 Pte Gibb } Nº 50601 Sgt ARLISS Wounded	

J.D. Matcliff Capt
Cmdg 6 M.G. Sqdn

WAR DIARY
or
INTELLIGENCE SUMMARY
(Erase heading not required.)

Army Form C. 2118

6 M.G. Squadron

January 1918

W.D. 23

Place	Date	Hour	Summary of Events and Information	Remarks and references to Appendices
EPAGNE	14/1/18 to 27/1/18		The Squadron remained in billets. Cleaning up after their spell in the trenches. Remounts were trained in their section. Football competition opened - A subsection beating B. (second). On 27th the Squadron received orders to march to MONCHY LAGACHE AREA and to relieve the 5th Division. S. Feb. 1st	
ARGOEUVRES	28/1/18		The Brigade marched to BELLOY. The Squadron billeted the night at ARGOEUVRES. distance 33 k	
HARBONNIERS	29/1/18		The Brigade marched to ROYART Area. The Squadron billets the night at HARBONNIERS. Distance 38 k.	
TERTRY	30/1/18		The Brigade marched to TERTRY. 82k The Squadron took over permanent billets 500 x y of TERTRY from the 14th M.G. Squadron Billets consist of NISSEN Huts and 1 ADRIAN HUT. Standings have been built for the horses.	
	31/1/18			

H.B. Ratcliffe Capt.
Commanding 6 M.G. Squadron

WAR DIARY
or
INTELLIGENCE SUMMARY

(Erase heading not required.)

Army Form C. 2118

(a Machine Gun Sqn.)

Vol 24

Place	Date	Hour	Summary of Events and Information	Remarks and references to Appendices
TERTRY	1/2/18 to 20/2/18		This period was spent in cleaning up the billeting area, erecting accommodation for men and horses, and supplying digging parties with the remainder of the Brigade for digging new trenches in rear of the present front line system. An average of 30 men was found daily. A gymkhana was started.	
	4/2/18		No 50537 S.S.M. WALKER. J awarded Croix de Guerre (Belgian). Captain C. D. LEYLAND (1st Life Gds) 7th M.G Squadron assumed command of this Squadron.	
	6/2/18			
	21/2/18		All ranks and 8 guns under Lt. G.H. EATON proceeded to trenches to position in and about JEANCOURT.	
	23/2/18		On the night Feb 25th/26th the 8 guns under Lt G.H. EATON were ordered to support a raid by the Canadian Cavalry Brigade (Fort Garry Horse). Position was taken up in LE DUC TRENCH (M.G od 2.2 of BELLENGLISE sheet 7/10,000) the relieving party sent Heyland Capt

WAR DIARY
or
INTELLIGENCE SUMMARY
(Erase heading not required.)

Army Form C. 2118

[?] H
(Machine Gun Sec.)

Place	Date	Hour	Summary of Events and Information	Remarks and references to Appendices
	21/7/18		over about 9.50 p.m. entering the houses and cellars about M 10 a.5.5. and penetrating some 500' down St HELENE'S TRENCH. Our barrage was put down on the German support line from M4 to central M5–C.9.2. About 2000 rounds were fired. Lt. J. D. BICKERSTETH was re-posted to ROYAL DRAGOONS and ceased to belong to M.G.C. Cavalry.	

Reynaud Cpl.

Army Form C. 2118

WAR DIARY
or
INTELLIGENCE SUMMARY

Sub #2 Machine Gun Squadron

Vol 25

(Erase heading not required.)

Instructions regarding War Diaries and Intelligence Summaries are contained in F.S. Regs., Part II. and the Staff Manual respectively. Title Pages will be prepared in manuscript.

Place	Date	Hour	Summary of Events and Information	Remarks and references to Appendices
TERTRY	3/3/18		Trench party under Lt. G. H. EATON returned from JEANCOURT area.	A.H.E.
	4/3/18		Brigade ordered to "Stand to" at 3 hours notice. Duty Subsection at ½ hours notice.	A.H.E.
	5/3/18		Squadron paraded for Brigade Scheme on hillside N.E. of TERTRY.	A.H.E.
	6/3/18		Gun, signalling and range finding classes for Sub sections.	A.H.E.
DEVISE	13/3/18		Squadron marched to DEVISE (distance 3½ miles). Lt. S.G. HIBBERT, 2ⁿᵈ Lt. C.C. SMITH and 7 other ranks transferred to 11th M.G. Squadron. Lt. A.G. WINDHAM and 16 O.R. arrived from 11th M.G. Squadron.	A.H.E.
	16/3/18		Capt. J.C. HUMFREY assumed command of the Squadron.	A.H.E.
	17/3/18		Final of Bgde. Inter Squadron Football Competition, won by 6th M.G. Squadron. Brig. General A.E.W. HARMAN presented medals to winning team.	
	21/3/18		Capt. J.C. HUMFREY departed on one month's leave to England. Squadron "standing to" at 1½ hours notice. Squadron moved off at 4.30 p.m. under Capt. T.B. RATCLIFFE. Arrived BEAUVOIR 11 p.m. Moved at 11.30 p.m. to vicinity of CHAUNY, and embussed for trenches by VIRY. Strength Capt. T.B. RATCLIFFE. 5 S. officers. 12 Guns. 5 men per gun.	

A.W. Ellis, Lt.

WAR DIARY
or
INTELLIGENCE SUMMARY

Army Form C. 2118

(Erase heading not required.)

Place	Date	Hour	Summary of Events and Information	Remarks and references to Appendices
VIRY	22/3/18		Took up position in reserve line at dawn. Sector held by 3rd D.Gs. Royals & 10th H.	A.w.s.
	23/3/18		Subjected to severe shelling. Infantry reported retiring on both flanks. Four guns ordered to support infantry on left flank & took up position midst heavy shelling. M.G. & rifle fire. Trench & own infantry retired, guns isolated. Lt. WILKES seriously wounded, one gun out of action. Two gunners killed & one wounded. Retired to ridge about 1 mile distant. Ridge abandoned & position taken up on sunken road N. of CHAUNY. Of the 8 guns under Capt F.B. RATCLIFFE two were withdrawn to village of VIRY.	A.w.s.
CHAUNY	24/3/18		All Squadron guns (10) assembled on sunken road N. of CHAUNY & took up positions with 3rd D.Gs. Royals & 10th H. Guns had good targets, but were forced to retire owing to enfilade fire from flanks. Capt. F.B. RATCLIFFE seriously wounded.	A.w.s.

Army Form C. 2118

WAR DIARY
or
INTELLIGENCE SUMMARY [April 1918] 6 Machine Gun [Squadron]

(Erase heading not required.)

Instructions regarding War Diaries and Intelligence Summaries are contained in F. S. Regs., Part II. and the Staff Manual respectively. Title Pages will be prepared in manuscript.

Place	Date	Hour	Summary of Events and Information	Remarks and references to Appendices
			Next position taken up about 500x of sunken road on high ground & held until evening, then fell back to trench line in ABBECOURT. Trench line held for one hour then withdrew to southern bank of canal at QUIERZY. LT. G. H. EATON killed night of 24/25 at QUIERZY.	H. M. G.
	24/3/18		Relieved by infantry & withdrew to support.	H. M. G.
			Night of 25/26 relieved from support & marched to billets at OLLENCOURT.	H. M. G.
CHOISY-AU-BAC	27/3/18		Led horses arrived & Squadron marched to wood S. of CHOISY-AU-BAC.	H. M. G.
	29/3/18		Marched from CHOISY-AU-BAC to ARION.	H. M. G.
	30/3/18		Marched to wood near SAINS-EN-AMIÉNOIS.	

H. M. Ellis M.

6th Cav.Bde.
3rd Cav.Div.

WAR
DIARY

6th MACHINE GUN SQUADRON.

A P R I L

1 9 1 8

Vol 26

Place	Date	Hour	Summary of Events and Information	Remarks and references to Appendices
E of BOVES	April 1st & 2nd		Squadron marched from SAINS-EN-AMIENOIS to woods about 1½ miles E of BOVES, where the Brigade bivouaced.	A+E
	3/4/18		Four guns marched to FOUILLY with 10th R. HUSSARS. 3rd D.Gds, Royals & remainder of machine guns moved to BOIS L'ABBE.	A+E
	4/4/18		Enemy attacked & 10th R.H. moved up in support of 14th Division taking up a position near sunken road 1 mile W of HAMEL. The other guns took up positions with 3rd D.Gds & Royals N of VILLERS-BRETONNEUX road & S.W. of B'de VAIRE. Guns with 10th R.H. relieved night of 4th + 5th by Australians.	A+E
	5/4/18		Guns with 10th R.H. took up positions on left of 3rd D.Gs. The regiments were relieved by Australians, night of 5th + 6th, but machine guns remained in positions.	A+E
	6/4/18		The Squadron was relieved by Australian machine guns night of 6th + 7th.	A+E

Place	Date	Hour	Summary of Events and Information	Remarks and references to Appendices
CAMON	7/4/18		Relief carried out & Squadron marched to billets at CAMON. The following officers joined the squadron. LT. HAWKINGS, 2LT. NEALE. 2LT. ELLIKER & 2LT. FLETCHER.	
	10/4/18 to		Squadron marched north to AUMERVAL passing through the following places :— BACHIMONT. CONTEVILLE. BAILLEUL-LES-PERNES. AUMERVAL	
AUMERVAL	30/4/18			

he OC 6th Machine Gun Squadron

Army Form C. 2118

WAR DIARY
~~INTELLIGENCE SUMMARY~~
(Erase heading not required.)

1st Machine Gun Squadron

Nov 27

Place	Date	Hour	Summary of Events and Information	Remarks and references to Appendices
AUMERVAL	12/3 4/4/16		Brigade was "standing to", but training was carried out near billets.	A.W.E.
	4/5 4/4/16		Brigade marched to new billeting area at CONTAY. Squadron marched via MONCHEL + BOFFLES.	A.W.E.
CONTAY	6/4/16 to 16/4/16		Brigade was standing to — saddling up by 5am every morning, except when regiments were digging. Reconnaissance of tracks + gun positions carried out by officers.	A.W.E.
BELLOY	17/4/16 to 30/4/16		Brigade moved to new area at BELLOY. Men + horses in wood N.E. of village. Intense training was carried out; staff rides for officers.	A.W.E.
MONTIGNY	31/4/16		Brigade moved to BEHENCOURT area, as duty Brigade, relieving 7th Brigade. Brigade "standing to" at 1½ hrs notice.	A.W.E.

J.C. Humfrey Capt.

Army Form C. 2118

WAR DIARY
or
INTELLIGENCE SUMMARY
(Erase heading not required.)

Machine Gun Corps
Sheet #5

Vol 28

Place	Date	Hour	Summary of Events and Information	Remarks and references to Appendices
MONTIGNY.	1-6-18 to 13-6-18		Brigade was "standing to". Reconnaissance of tracks & Machine Gun positions by sub section officers.	t.w.E
BELLOY	14-6-18 to 24-6-18		Brigade moved to BELLOY where programme of training was carried out.	t.w.E
RIENCOURT.	25-6-18		Squadron moved to new area at RIENCOURT. Ordinary camp routine.	t.w.E

J.C. Humphrey, Major
COMMANDING 6th MACHINE

WAR DIARY
or
INTELLIGENCE SUMMARY

Army Form C. 2118

(Erase heading not required.)

Place	Date	Hour	Summary of Events and Information	Remarks and references to Appendices
RIENCOURT	1.7.18 to 31.7.18		The Squadron carried out Lanagin training	

J.C.Heun for Major
Comdg 6 M.G. Sqn.

Army Form C. 2118

6th M.G. Sqdn

Sheet 50.

VII 30

WAR DIARY
or
INTELLIGENCE SUMMARY
(Erase heading not required.)

Instructions regarding War Diaries and Intelligence Summaries are contained in F. S. Regs., Part II. and the Staff Manual respectively. Title Pages will be prepared in manuscript.

Aug.

Place	Date	Hour	Summary of Events and Information	Remarks and references to Appendices
RIENCOURT	1-9-18 to 4-9-18		Ordinary Camp routine.	4. M. G.
LE MESGE	5-9-18		Squadron moved to LE MESGE (Night March)	4. M. G.
PETIT ST JEAN	6-9-18		Brigade moved to PONT-DE-METZ area. (Night March.)	4. M. G.
	7-9-18		Brigade moved forward by night to Concentration Area N.E. of BOVES.	4. M. G.
	8-9-18		Brigade advanced in support of 7th Brigade through DEMUIN & finally took up a position along the old AMIEN defence line, holding the valley & road one mile S. of CAIX on CAIX, LE QUESNEL Road.	4. M. G.
	9-9-18		Squadron was relieved at 11am & came back with 3rd Division into Corps Reserve W. of CAIX.	4. M. G.
	10-9-18		Brigade moved forward & followed the infantry. Bivouaced the same night E. of FOLIES.	4. M. G.
	11-9-18		5 P.M. Brigade moved back to billets at FOUENCAMPS	4. M. G.
RIENCOURT	12-9-18		Squadron moved back to previous billets at RIENCOURT.	4. M. G.

Army Form C. 2118

WAR DIARY
or
INTELLIGENCE SUMMARY
(Erase heading not required.)

Sheet 57.

Place	Date	Hour	Summary of Events and Information	Remarks and references to Appendices
RIENCOURT	16 to 21.9.18		Ordinary billet routine. Squadron moved to billets at FIEFFS.	A.M.E
FIEFFS	22 to 25.9.18		Ordinary billet routine. Moved to WILLENCOURT.	
	26.9.18		Moved to billets at GRAND BOURET.	
	29.9.18		Four guns under Lieut SANDERS moved forward with the 10th Royal Hussars to the ARRAS front but did not go into action.	A.M.E

J.C.Chamberlayne
Capt. 10th Hussars.

Army Form C. 2118.

WAR DIARY
INTELLIGENCE SUMMARY
(Erase heading not required.)

Place	Date	Hour	Summary of Events and Information	Remarks and references to Appendices
GRAND BOURET	Sept 14		Billet Routine	JCH
WILLEMAN	Sept 15		I.S.O. returns from Wailly with 10th Hussars	JCH
	Sept 16		Moved billets to WILLEMAN	JCH
	Sept 17			JCH
	Sept 17		Moved out for manoeuvres round BOIS LE CHATEAU	
NUNCQ	Sept 18		Moved to NUNCQ	NCH
ST LEGER	Sept 19		Moved to ST LEGER	JCH
ALBERT AREA	Sept 20		Moved to MEAULT	ALBERT
HEM	Sept 21		Arr'd HEM	JCH
VERMAND	Sept 21		Moved to VERMAND	JCH
	Sept 22		Billet routine	JCH

WAR DIARY / INTELLIGENCE SUMMARY

Army Form C. 2118

October 1918
6 Machine Gun Sqn

No. 32

Place	Date	Hour	Summary of Events and Information	Remarks and references
VERMAND BELLENGLISE VERMAND	Oct 1	08.00	Squadron bivouacked at VERMAND on an hours notice. MH	
	2	13.40	Returned to VERMAND " marched to BELLENGLISE assembly area — objective LE CATEAU. MH	
BELLENGLISE PONTRUET	3	10 to 16 00	Marched to BELLENGLISE MH. at H.20. Central when Squadron halted came under machine gun fire from Advanced Valley 62.B.20.00. Aeroplanes & also slight shelling from light artillery. Returned to PONTRUET at 16.00.2. MH	
TREFCON G.30.C.57B U.12.	4 5 6 7	10.30 04.00 17.00 16.00	PONTRUET. MH marched to TREFCON. MH at G.30.C. marched to a point about 10.0 x south of BEAUREVOIR. to starting point; 62.B. H40,000. MH Returned to assembly area MH Marched to 57B.20,00 U.12.b. Two guns under Lt NEALE attached to 3rd Dragoon Guards came into action at P.23d. with great effect on enemy retiring. Later engaged a light field gun withdrawing support at 2000 yards and 2/Lt ELLIS attached to 1st Royal Dragoons came into action but did not fire as enemy retired. Our guns with their officers & two gun numbers knocked out by a shell — at 57.B. 40,000. P.24.a. Two guns under Lt. YOUNGHUSBAND attached to 10th Hussars. Came into action against aeroplanes when attacked by them & drove them off. MH Remainder of Squadron moved to V.I.d. and came under heavy shellfire — returned to V.I.P. Later moved with main body of Brigade to V.2. where they were heavily engaged by aeroplanes with bombs & M.G. fire — Six guns came into action & drove enemy off — later moved to HONNECHY to P.23. Central coming under heavy shell fire from the G. fork. Stormed Cavalletio Kiosk & forked. MH	
P.23.d.		17 00	All guns came into action at Southern part of P.23.d. to cover flank of Cavalry advancing on LE CATEAU from about P.23.b. Advanced did not take place but two guns under 2/Lt ELLIKER opened fire with good effect on enemy M.Gs & Infantry digging in at a range of 1100 x about 400 yds front. at dusk Squadron returned to P.23.b. during the night enemy shelled forces around Cavaletio Secourt. MH 2/Lt 30.C. slightly shelled there. Returned to MONTIGNY that afternoon. MH	
MONTIGNY ELINCOURT	10 11	05 00	Marched to P.5. central — 57 30.C. slightly shelled there. MH Marched to HOTEL ELINCOURT. MH	

Army Form C. 2118

WAR DIARY
or
INTELLIGENCE SUMMARY
(Erase heading not required.)

October 1915
6 Machine Gun Section

Place	Date	Hour	Summary of Events and Information	Remarks and references to Appendices
BANTEUX	13th		Moved to BANTEUX.	
ETRICOURT	14		" " ETRICOURT.	
EQUANCOURT	23 to 31st		" " EQUANCOURT.	

J C Humfrey Major
Cmdg VI Th C. M Gun Sn.

Army Form C. 2118

6th Machine Gun Sqn
NOVEMBER 1918

Vol 33

WAR DIARY
INTELLIGENCE SUMMARY
(Erase heading not required.)

Place	Date	Hour	Summary of Events and Information	Remarks and references to Appendices
EQUANCOURT	1st Nov. 6th Nov.		At EQUANCOURT. HWL	
SANS-LEZ-MARQUION	6th "		Moved to SANS-LEZ-MARQUION HWL	
ESQUERCHIN	7th		" " ESQUERCHIN. HWL	
PERONNE	8th		" " PÉRONNE HWL	
VAULX-la-TOURNAI	10th		" " VAULX-la-TOURNAI. HWL	
"	11th		Squadron moved up to LEUZE — 2 subsections joined each regiment — rejoined returned billets in the evening — HWL	
BERTINCROIX	13th		Moved to BERTINCROIX. HWL	
FOULENG	17th		" " FOULENG "B" subsection joined 3rd D. Gds. "D" subsection to the "Royals". HWL	
QUENAST	18th		" " QUENAST. HWL	
LIMELETTE	21st		" " LIMELETTE. "E" subsection joined the Xth Hussars. HWL	
GRAND ROSIERE	22nd		" " GRAND ROSIERE. HWL	
LES BOSCAILLES	24th to 30th		" " LES BOSCAILLES. HWL	

J C Hunter
Major
Commanding 6th Machine Gun Squadron

6 M.G Sqn
Vol 34

WAR DIARY — DECEMBER 1918.
6TH M.G. SQUADRON. IN THE FIELD.

DATES	PLACE		
Dec 1st	Les Bascailles	The Squadron moved to billets in LEUZE	JCH
10th	LEUZE	The Squadron moved to FUMAL	JCH
12th	FUMAL	The Squadron moved to YERNAWE	JCH
20th to present date	YERNAWE	The Squadron moved to AMAY	JCH

J C Humphreys Major
Comdg 6th M.G. Sqdn.

6 M.G. Squad

WAR DIARY.

WO 95/

A.I.F.

PLACE	DATE	
Amay	Jany 8 to Feby 8	In Billets at Amay.

A.W.Grantham. Capt.
Commanding 6th Machine Gun Squadron

8/2/19

6th MACHINE GUN SQUADRON. War Diary for February. 1919.

Vol 36

DATE	PLACE.	RECORD OF EVENTS	Feb: Aug̃w.
Feb: 1st to Feb: 28th	Amay	In billets at Amay	

Aughrandham Capt.
for Major Comdg. 6th M.G. Squadron

11-3-19

3 Cav

6th Machine Gun Squadron. 14. War Diary for March 1919. Vol 37

Date.	Place.	Record of Events.	
Mar. 1st to Mar. 14th	Amay	In billets	a.b.
Mar. 14th		Squadron moved to St. Georges.	a.b.
" 14th to Mar. 31st	St. Georges	In billets	a.b.

8/4/19

A Cooper Lt. for
Major
Cmdg. 6th M.G.S.

6th M.G. Squadron

War Diary April 1919.

Vol 38

Date	Place	Record of Events.	Initials of Officer
April 1st to April 30th	St. Georges.	In Billets.	JCA

J C Churchey
Major.
COMMANDING 6th MACHINE GUN SQUADRON.

WAR DIARY
or
INTELLIGENCE SUMMARY

Army Form C. 2118

6 M G Sqn Vol 39

Place	Date	Hour	Summary of Events and Information	Remarks and references to Appendices
AMR 1	May 1st to May 29		Billet routine	J.A.

J C Hewn Fryburg
Capt II CH Sqn

www.ingramcontent.com/pod-product-compliance
Lightning Source LLC
Chambersburg PA
CBHW081241170426
43191CB00034B/2000